RENAL DIET COOKBOOK

MEGA BUNDLE – 3 Manuscripts in 1 – 120+ Renal - friendly recipes including smoothies, pies, and pancakes for a delicious and tasty diet

TABLE OF CONTENTS

This document is geared towards providing exact and reliable information in regards to the topic and issue covered. The publication is sold with the idea that the publisher is not required to render accounting, officially permitted, or otherwise, qualified services. If advice is necessary, legal or professional, a practiced individual in the profession should be ordered.

- From a Declaration of Principles which was accepted and approved equally by a Committee of the American Bar Association and a Committee of Publishers and Associations.

The information provided herein is stated to be truthful and consistent, in that any liability, in terms of inattention or otherwise, by any usage or abuse of any policies, processes, or directions contained within is the solitary and utter responsibility of the recipient reader. Under no circumstances will any legal responsibility or blame be held against the publisher for any reparation, damages, or monetary loss due to the information herein, either directly or indirectly.

The information herein is offered for informational purposes solely, and is universal as so. The presentation of the information is without contract or any type of guarantee assurance.

The trademarks that are used are without any consent, and the publication of the trademark is without permission or backing by the trademark owner. All trademarks and brands within this book are for clarifying purposes only and are the owned by the owners themselves, not affiliated with this document.

Introduction

Renal   recipes for personal enjoyment but also for family enjoyment. You will love them for sure for how easy it is to prepare them.

BLUEBERRY PANCAKES

Serves: **4**

Prep Time: **10**   Minutes

Cook Time: **20**   Minutes

Total Time: **30**   Minutes

INGREDIENTS

- 1 cup whole wheat flour
- ¼ tsp baking soda
- ¼ tsp baking powder
- 1 cup blueberries
- 2 eggs
- 1 cup milk

DIRECTIONS

1. In a bowl combine all ingredients together and mix well
2. In a skillet heat olive oil
3. Pour ¼ of the batter and cook each pancake for 1-2 minutes per side
4. When ready remove from heat and serve

Serves: **4**

Prep Time: **10** Minutes

Cook Time: **30** Minutes

Total Time: **40** Minutes

INGREDIENTS

- 1 cup whole wheat flour
- ¼ tsp baking soda
- ¼ tsp baking powder
- 1 cup apples
- 2 eggs
- 1 cup milk

DIRECTIONS

1. In a bowl combine all ingredients together and mix well
2. In a skillet heat olive oil
3. Pour ¼ of the batter and cook each pancake for 1-2 minutes per side
4. When ready remove from heat and serve

BANANA PANCAKES

Serves: **4**

Prep Time: **10** Minutes

Cook Time: **20** Minutes

Total Time: **30** Minutes

INGREDIENTS

- 1 cup whole wheat flour
- ¼ tsp baking soda
- ¼ tsp baking powder
- 1 cup mashed banana
- 2 eggs
- 1 cup milk

DIRECTIONS

1. In a bowl combine all ingredients together and mix well
2. In a skillet heat olive oil
3. Pour ¼ of the batter and cook each pancake for 1-2 minutes per side
4. When ready remove from heat and serve

Serves: **4**

Prep Time: **10**   Minutes

Cook Time: **20**   Minutes

Total Time: **30**   Minutes

INGREDIENTS

- 1 cup whole wheat flour
- ¼ tsp baking soda
- ¼ tsp baking powder
- 1 cup apricots
- 2 eggs
- 1 cup milk

DIRECTIONS

1. In a bowl combine all ingredients together and mix well
2. In a skillet heat olive oil
3. Pour ¼ of the batter and cook each pancake for 1-2 minutes per side
4. When ready remove from heat and serve

PANCAKES

Serves: *4*

Prep Time: *10*   Minutes

Cook Time: *30*   Minutes

Total Time: *40*   Minutes

INGREDIENTS

- 1 cup whole wheat flour
- ¼ tsp baking soda
- ¼ tsp baking powder
- 2 eggs
- 1 cup milk

DIRECTIONS

1. In a bowl combine all ingredients together and mix well
2. In a skillet heat olive oil
3. Pour ¼ of the batter and cook each pancake for 1-2 minutes per side
4. When ready remove from heat and serve

CRANBERRIES MUFFINS

Serves: *8-12*

Prep Time: *10*   Minutes

Cook Time: *20*   Minutes

Total Time: *30*   Minutes

INGREDIENTS

- 2 eggs
- 1 tablespoon olive oil
- 1 cup milk
- 2 cups whole wheat flour
- 1 tsp baking soda
- ¼ tsp baking soda
- 1 tsp ginger
- ½ cup cranberries
- ¼ cup molasses

DIRECTIONS

1. In a bowl combine all wet ingredients
2. In another bowl combine all dry ingredients
3. Combine wet and dry ingredients together
4. Pour mixture into 8-12 prepared muffin cups, fill 2/3 of the cups
5. Bake for 18-20 minutes at 375 F

DURIAN MUFFINS

Serves: **8-12**

Prep Time: **10** Minutes

Cook Time: **20** Minutes

Total Time: **30** Minutes

INGREDIENTS

- 2 eggs
- 1 tablespoon olive oil
- 1 cup milk
- 2 cups whole wheat flour
- 1 tsp baking soda
- ¼ tsp baking soda
- 1 tsp cinnamon
- 1 cup durian

DIRECTIONS

1. In a bowl combine all wet ingredients
2. In another bowl combine all dry ingredients
3. Combine wet and dry ingredients together
4. Pour mixture into 8-12 prepared muffin cups, fill 2/3 of the cups
5. Bake for 18-20 minutes at 375 F
6. When ready remove from the oven and serve

BLUEBERRY MUFFINS

Serves: *8-12*
Prep Time: *10*   Minutes

Cook Time: *20*   Minutes

Total Time: *30*   Minutes

INGREDIENTS

- 2 eggs
- 1 tablespoon olive oil
- 1 cup milk
- 2 cups whole wheat flour
- 1 tsp baking soda
- ¼ tsp baking soda
- 1 tsp cinnamon
- 1 cup blueberries

DIRECTIONS

1. In a bowl combine all wet ingredients
2. In another bowl combine all dry ingredients
3. Combine wet and dry ingredients together
4. Fold in blueberries and mix well
5. Pour mixture into 8-12 prepared muffin cups, fill 2/3 of the cups
6. Bake for 18-20 minutes at 375 F

FEIJOA MUFFINS

Serves: **8-12**

Prep Time: **10** Minutes

Cook Time: **20** Minutes

Total Time: **30** Minutes

INGREDIENTS

- 2 eggs
- 1 tablespoon olive oil
- 1 cup milk
- 2 cups whole wheat flour
- 1 tsp baking soda
- ¼ tsp baking soda
- 1 tsp cinnamon
- 1 cup feijoa

DIRECTIONS

1. In a bowl combine all wet ingredients
2. In another bowl combine all dry ingredients
3. Combine wet and dry ingredients together
4. Pour mixture into 8-12 prepared muffin cups, fill 2/3 of the cups
5. Bake for 18-20 minutes at 375 F
6. When ready remove from the oven and serve

KIWI MUFFINS

Serves: **8-12**

Prep Time: **10** Minutes

Cook Time: **20** Minutes

Total Time: **30** Minutes

INGREDIENTS

- 2 eggs
- 1 tablespoon olive oil
- 1 cup milk
- 2 cups whole wheat flour
- 1 tsp baking soda
- ¼ tsp baking soda
- 1 tsp cinnamon
- 1 cup kiwi

DIRECTIONS

1. In a bowl combine all wet ingredients
2. In another bowl combine all dry ingredients
3. Combine wet and dry ingredients together
4. Pour mixture into 8-12 prepared muffin cups, fill 2/3 of the cups
5. Bake for 18-20 minutes at 375 F
6. When ready remove from the oven and serve

Serves: **8-12**
Prep Time: **10**   Minutes

Cook Time: **20**   Minutes

Total Time: **30**   Minutes

INGREDIENTS

- 2 eggs
- 1 tablespoon olive oil
- 1 cup milk
- 2 cups whole wheat flour
- 1 tsp baking soda
- ¼ tsp baking soda
- 1 tsp cinnamon

DIRECTIONS

1. In a bowl combine all wet ingredients
2. In another bowl combine all dry ingredients
3. Combine wet and dry ingredients together
4. Pour mixture into 8-12 prepared muffin cups, fill 2/3 of the cups
5. Bake for 18-20 minutes at 375 F
6. When ready remove from the oven and serve

GOAT CHEESE OMELETTE

Serves: **1**
Prep Time: **5**   Minutes

Cook Time: **10**   Minutes

Total Time: **15**   Minutes

INGREDIENTS

- 2 eggs
- ¼ tsp salt
- ¼ tsp black pepper
- 1 tablespoon olive oil
- ¼ cup goat cheese
- ¼ tsp basil

DIRECTIONS

1. In a bowl combine all ingredients together and mix well
2. In a skillet heat olive oil and pour the egg mixture
3. Cook for 1-2 minutes per side
4. When ready remove omelette from the skillet and serve

BACON OMELETTE

Serves: *1*

Prep Time: *5*   Minutes

Cook Time: *10*   Minutes

Total Time: *15*   Minutes

INGREDIENTS

- 2 eggs
- ¼ tsp salt
- ¼ tsp black pepper
- 1 tablespoon olive oil
- ½ cup bacon
- ¼ tsp basil
- 1 cup zucchini

DIRECTIONS

1. In a bowl combine all ingredients together and mix well
2. In a skillet heat olive oil and pour the egg mixture
3. Cook for 1-2 minutes per side
4. When ready remove omelette from the skillet and serve

Serves: *1*
Prep Time: *5*   Minutes

Cook Time: *10*   Minutes

Total Time: *15*   Minutes

INGREDIENTS

- 2 eggs
- ¼ tsp salt
- ¼ tsp black pepper
- 1 tablespoon olive oil
- ¼ cup cheese
- ¼ tsp basil
- 1 cup red onion

DIRECTIONS

1. In a bowl combine all ingredients together and mix well
2. In a skillet heat olive oil and pour the egg mixture
3. Cook for 1-2 minutes per side
4. When ready remove omelette from the skillet and serve

FETA CHEESE OMELETTE

Serves: *1*
Prep Time: *5*   Minutes

Cook Time: *10*   Minutes

Total Time: *15*   Minutes

INGREDIENTS

- 2 eggs
- ¼ tsp salt
- ¼ tsp black pepper
- 1 tablespoon olive oil
- ¼ cup cheese
- ¼ tsp basil
- ½ cup feta cheese

DIRECTIONS

1. In a bowl combine all ingredients together and mix well
2. In a skillet heat olive oil and pour the egg mixture
3. Cook for 1-2 minutes per side
4. When ready remove omelette from the skillet and serve

TOMATO OMELETTE

Serves: *1*
Prep Time: 5 Minutes

Cook Time: *10* Minutes

Total Time: *15* Minutes

INGREDIENTS

- 2 eggs
- ¼ tsp salt
- ¼ tsp black pepper
- 1 tablespoon olive oil
- ¼ cup cheese
- ¼ tsp basil
- 1 cup tomatoes

DIRECTIONS

1. In a bowl combine all ingredients together and mix well
2. In a skillet heat olive oil and pour the egg mixture
3. Cook for 1-2 minutes per side
4. When ready remove omelette from the skillet and serve

BEANS OMELETTE

Serves: *1*

Prep Time: *5*   Minutes

Cook Time: *10*   Minutes

Total Time: *15*   Minutes

INGREDIENTS

- 2 eggs
- ¼ tsp salt
- ¼ tsp black pepper
- 1 tablespoon olive oil
- ¼ cup cheese
- ¼ tsp basil
- 1 cup beans

DIRECTIONS

1. In a bowl combine all ingredients together and mix well
2. In a skillet heat olive oil and pour the egg mixture
3. Cook for 1-2 minutes per side
4. When ready remove omelette from the skillet and serve

Serves: 2

Prep Time: 5   Minutes

Cook Time: 30   Minutes

Total Time: 35   Minutes

INGREDIENTS

- 1 tsp vanilla extract
- 1 tablespoon honey
- 1 lb. rolled oats
- 2 tablespoons sesame seeds
- ¼ lb. almonds
- ¼ lb. berries

DIRECTIONS

1. Preheat the oven to 325 F
2. Spread the granola onto a baking sheet
3. Bake for 12-15 minutes, remove and mix everything
4. Bake for another 12-15 minutes or until slightly brown
5. When ready remove from the oven and serve

Serves: **4**

Prep Time: **10**   Minutes

Cook Time: **20**   Minutes

Total Time: **30**   Minutes

INGREDIENTS

- 1 cup whole wheat flour
- ¼ tsp baking soda
- ¼ tsp baking powder
- 1 cup blueberries
- 2 eggs
- 1 cup milk

DIRECTIONS

1. In a bowl combine all ingredients together and mix well
2. In a skillet heat olive oil
3. Pour ¼ of the batter and cook each pancake for 1-2 minutes per side
4. When ready remove from heat and serve

APPLE PANCAKES

Serves: **4**

Prep Time: **10**   Minutes

Cook Time: **30**   Minutes

Total Time: **40**   Minutes

INGREDIENTS

- 1 cup whole wheat flour
- ¼ tsp baking soda
- ¼ tsp baking powder
- 1 cup apples
- 2 eggs
- 1 cup milk

DIRECTIONS

1. In a bowl combine all ingredients together and mix well
2. In a skillet heat olive oil
3. Pour ¼ of the batter and cook each pancake for 1-2 minutes per side
4. When ready remove from heat and serve

BANANA PANCAKES

Serves: **4**

Prep Time: **10**   Minutes

Cook Time: **20**   Minutes

Total Time: **30**   Minutes

INGREDIENTS

- 1 cup whole wheat flour
- ¼ tsp baking soda
- ¼ tsp baking powder
- 1 cup mashed banana
- 2 eggs
- 1 cup milk

DIRECTIONS

1. In a bowl combine all ingredients together and mix well
2. In a skillet heat olive oil
3. Pour ¼ of the batter and cook each pancake for 1-2 minutes per side
4. When ready remove from heat and serve

APRICOTS PANCAKES

Serves: **4**

Prep Time: **10** Minutes

Cook Time: **20** Minutes

Total Time: **30** Minutes

INGREDIENTS

- 1 cup whole wheat flour
- ¼ tsp baking soda
- ¼ tsp baking powder
- 1 cup apricots
- 2 eggs
- 1 cup milk

DIRECTIONS

1. In a bowl combine all ingredients together and mix well
2. In a skillet heat olive oil
3. Pour ¼ of the batter and cook each pancake for 1-2 minutes per side
4. When ready remove from heat and serve

PANCAKES

Serves: *4*
Prep Time: *10*   Minutes

Cook Time: *30*   Minutes

Total Time: *40*   Minutes

INGREDIENTS

- 1 cup whole wheat flour
- ¼ tsp baking soda
- ¼ tsp baking powder
- 2 eggs
- 1 cup milk

DIRECTIONS

1. In a bowl combine all ingredients together and mix well
2. In a skillet heat olive oil
3. Pour ¼ of the batter and cook each pancake for 1-2 minutes per side
4. When ready remove from heat and serve

Serves: **1**

Prep Time: **5**   Minutes

Cook Time: **5**   Minutes

Total Time: **10**   Minutes

INGREDIENTS

- ½ cup dried raisins
- ½ cup dried pecans
- ¼ cup almonds
- 1 cup coconut milk
- 1 tsp cinnamon

DIRECTIONS

1. In a bowl combine all ingredients together
2. Serve with milk

Serves: 2

Prep Time: 5   Minutes

Cook Time: 15   Minutes

Total Time: 20   Minutes

INGREDIENTS

- ¼ cup egg substitute
- 1 muffin
- 1 turkey sausage patty
- 1 tablespoon cheddar cheese

DIRECTIONS

1. In a skillet pour egg and cook on low heat
2. Place turkey sausage patty in a pan and cook for 4-5 minutes per side
3. On a toasted muffin place the cooked egg, top with a sausage patty and cheddar cheese
4. Serve when ready

DESSERTS

BREAKFAST COOKIES

Serves: **8-12**

Prep Time: 5 Minutes

Cook Time: **15** Minutes

Total Time: **20** Minutes

INGREDIENTS

- 1 cup rolled oats
- ¼ cup applesauce
- ½ tsp vanilla extract
- 3 tablespoons chocolate chips
- 2 tablespoons dried fruits
- 1 tsp cinnamon

DIRECTIONS

1. Preheat the oven to 325 F
2. In a bowl combine all ingredients together and mix well
3. Scoop cookies using an ice cream scoop
4. Place cookies onto a prepared baking sheet
5. Place in the oven for 12-15 minutes or until the cookies are done
6. When ready remove from the oven and serve

PEAR TART

Serves: *6-8*

Prep Time: **25**   Minutes

Cook Time: **25**   Minutes

Total Time: **50**   Minutes

INGREDIENTS

- 1 lb. pears
- 2 oz. brown sugar
- ½ lb. flaked almonds
- ¼ lb. porridge oat
- 2 oz. flour
- ¼ lb. almonds
- pastry sheets
- 2 tablespoons syrup

DIRECTIONS

1. Preheat oven to 400 F, unfold pastry sheets and place them on a baking sheet
2. Toss together all ingredients together and mix well
3. Spread mixture in a single layer on the pastry sheets
4. Before baking decorate with your desired fruits
5. Bake at 400 F for 22-25 minutes or until golden brown
6. When ready remove from the oven and serve

CARDAMOM TART

Serves: **6-8**
Prep Time: **25**   Minutes

Cook Time: **25**   Minutes

Total Time: **50**   Minutes

INGREDIENTS

- 4-5 pears
- 2 tablespoons lemon juice
- pastry sheets

CARDAMOM FILLING

- ½ lb. butter
- ½ lb. brown sugar
- ½ lb. almonds
- ¼ lb. flour
- 1 ¼ tsp cardamom
- 2 eggs

DIRECTIONS

1. Preheat oven to 400 F, unfold pastry sheets and place them on a baking sheet
2. Toss together all ingredients together and mix well
3. Spread mixture in a single layer on the pastry sheets
4. Before baking decorate with your desired fruits

5. Bake at 400 F for 22-25 minutes or until golden brown
6. When ready remove from the oven and serve

Serves:	**6-8**	
Prep Time:	**25**	Minutes
Cook Time:	**25**	Minutes
Total Time:	**50**	Minutes

INGREDIENTS

- pastry sheets

FILLING

- 1 tsp lemon juice
- 3 oz. brown sugar
- 1 lb. apples
- 150 ml double cream
- 2 eggs

DIRECTIONS

1. Preheat oven to 400 F, unfold pastry sheets and place them on a baking sheet
2. Toss together all ingredients together and mix well
3. Spread mixture in a single layer on the pastry sheets
4. Before baking decorate with your desired fruits
5. Bake at 400 F for 22-25 minutes or until golden brown
6. When ready remove from the oven and serve

SMOOTHIES AND DRINKS

BANANA BREAKFAST SMOOTHIE

Serves: **1**

Prep Time: **5**   Minutes

Cook Time: **5**   Minutes

Total Time: **10**   Minutes

INGREDIENTS

- ½ cup vanilla yogurt
- 2 tsp honey
- Pinch of cinnamon
- 1 banana
- 1 cup ice

DIRECTIONS

1. In a blender place all ingredients and blend until smooth
2. Pour the smoothie in a glass and serve

CINNAMON SMOOTHIE

Serves: **1**

Prep Time: **5** Minutes

Cook Time: **5** Minutes

Total Time: **10** Minutes

INGREDIENTS

- 1 cup soy milk
- 1 banana
- 1 tablespoon vanilla essence
- 1 cup strawberries
- ¼ tsp cinnamon

DIRECTIONS

1. In a blender place all ingredients and blend until smooth
2. Pour smoothie in a glass and serve

PEANUT BUTTER SMOOTHIE

Serves: **1**

Prep Time: **5**   Minutes

Cook Time: **5**   Minutes

Total Time: **10** Minutes

INGREDIENTS

- 1 cup soy milk
- 1 banana
- 1 tablespoon peanut butter
- ¼ tsp cinnamon
- 1 cup ice

DIRECTIONS

1. In a blender place all ingredients and blend until smooth
2. Pour smoothie in a glass and serve

SPINACH SMOOTHIE

Serves: *1*

Prep Time: 5   Minutes

Cook Time: 5   Minutes

Total Time: *10*   Minutes

INGREDIENTS

- 1 banana
- 1 cup ice
- ¼ cup blueberries
- 1 cup spinach

DIRECTIONS

1. In a blender place all ingredients and blend until smooth
2. Pour smoothie in a glass and serve

STRAWBERRY SMOOTHIE

Serves: **1**

Prep Time: **5** Minutes

Cook Time: **5** Minutes

Total Time: **10** Minutes

INGREDIENTS

- 1 cup strawberries
- 1 cup cranberry juice
- ½ cup orange juice
- 1 cup vanilla yogurt

DIRECTIONS

1. In a blender place all ingredients and blend until smooth
2. Pour smoothie in a glass and serve

Serves: **1**

Prep Time: **5** Minutes

Cook Time: **5** Minutes

Total Time: **10** Minutes

INGREDIENTS

- 2 bananas
- 2 tablespoons cocoa powder
- 1 tablespoon maple syrup
- ½ cup peanut butter
- 1 cup ice
- 2 cups almond milk

DIRECTIONS

1. In a blender place all ingredients and blend until smooth
2. Pour smoothie in a glass and serve

AVOCADO SMOOTHIE

Serves: **1**

Prep Time: **5**   Minutes

Cook Time: **5**   Minutes

Total Time: **10**   Minutes

INGREDIENTS

- 1 avocado
- 2 cups mango juice
- 1 cup orange juice
- 1 cup ice

DIRECTIONS

1. **In a blender place all ingredients and blend until smooth**
2. **Pour smoothie in a glass and serve**

LOW-CALORIE SMOOTHIE

Serves: *1*

Prep Time: *5*   Minutes

Cook Time: *5*   Minutes

Total Time: *10*   Minutes

INGREDIENTS

- 1 cup tomato juice
- ½ cup carrot juice
- 1 celery
- 1 cup spinach
- 1 cucumber
- 1 cup ice

DIRECTIONS

1. In a blender place all ingredients and blend until smooth
2. Pour smoothie in a glass and serve

BERRY SMOOTHIE

Serves: *1*

Prep Time: *5*   Minutes

Cook Time: *5*   Minutes

Total Time: *10*   Minutes

INGREDIENTS

- 1 cup strawberries
- 1 cup blueberries
- 1 cup yogurt
- 1 cup beet juice
- 1 cup ice

DIRECTIONS

1. In a blender place all ingredients and blend until smooth
2. Pour smoothie in a glass and serve

CARDAMOM SMOOTHIE

Serves: *1*
Prep Time: 5   Minutes

Cook Time: 5   Minutes

Total Time: *10*   Minutes

INGREDIENTS

- 1 banana
- 2 dates
- 1 cup Greek yogurt
- 1-inch ginger
- ½ cup coconut milk
- ½ tsp cardamom

DIRECTIONS

1. In a blender place all ingredients and blend until smooth
2. Pour smoothie in a glass and serve

SECOND COOKBOOK

MUSHROOM OMELETTE

Serves: *1*
Prep Time: 5   Minutes

Cook Time: *10*   Minutes

Total Time: *15*   Minutes

INGREDIENTS

- 2 eggs
- ¼ tsp salt
- ¼ tsp black pepper
- 1 tablespoon olive oil
- ¼ cup cheese
- ¼ tsp basil
- 1 cup mushrooms

DIRECTIONS

1. In a bowl combine all ingredients together and mix well
2. In a skillet heat olive oil and pour the egg mixture
3. Cook for 1-2 minutes per side
4. When ready remove omelette from the skillet and serve

Serves: **2**
Prep Time: **10** Minutes

Cook Time: **10** Minutes

Total Time: **20** Minutes

INGREDIENTS

- 2 eggs
- pinch of salt
- 1 tablespoon chives
- 1 tablespoon pesto
- bit of goat cheese
- handful of salad greens

DIRECTIONS

1. In a bowl beat eggs and pour in a skillet over medium heat, sprinkle with chives, and spread the pesto across the omelette
2. Sprinkle salad greens, cheese and season with salt

Serves: **6**
Prep Time: **10** Minutes

Cook Time: **10** Minutes

Total Time: **20** Minutes

INGREDIENTS

- ½ cup quinoa
- 1 tablespoon olive oil
- 1 onion
- 3 cups spinach leaves
- 1 garlic clove
- ¼ shallot
- salt
- ¼ cup cheddar cheese
- ¼ cup parmesan cheese
- 1 egg

DIRECTIONS

1. Preheat oven to 350 F and line a six-cup muffin pan
2. Combine water and quinoa in a saucepan and bring to boil
3. Lower the heat and cook for 12-15 minutes, remove from heat and allow to cool
4. In a skillet heat oil, add onion and cook for 4-5 minutes

5. Stir in shallot, garlic and spinach and season with salt and pepper
6. Remove the pan from heat and mix with quinoa, pour in the eggs
7. Divide the batter into muffin cups and bake for 30-35 minutes

Serves: *4*
Prep Time: *10* Minutes

Cook Time: *10* Minutes

Total Time: *20* Minutes

INGREDIENTS

- 10 cups
- ½ cup butter
- 1 cup diced celery
- ¼ cup onion
- 1 cup chopped cranberries
- ½ cup sugar
- 1 tsp sage
- 1 tsp rosemary
- 1 tsp sage
- 1 tsp rosemary
- 1 tsp thyme
- ½ cup parsley
- salt
- 1 lb. ground sausage
- 1 cup chicken broth

DIRECTIONS

1. In a saucepan heat butter over medium heat, add onion, celery and cook, add cranberries, sage, sugar, rosemary, parsley, thyme
2. Season with salt and pepper
3. Brown the sausage in a skillet, drain off fat
4. Toss the ingredients in the bowl and add chicken broth
5. Serve when ready

Serves: **6**
Prep Time: **10**   Minutes

Cook Time: **10**   Minutes

Total Time: **20**   Minutes

INGREDIENTS

- 10 oz. chopped kale
- 2 eggs
- 2 egg whites
- ½ cup leek
- ½ cup chopped tomato
- ½ cup bell pepper

DIRECTIONS

1. Preheat oven to 325 F and line a muffin pan with paper liners
2. In a bowl leek, egg whites, tomatoes, kale, eggs and bell pepper
3. Divide mixture into muffin cups and bake for 15-20 minutes
4. Remove and serve

Serves: **6**

Prep Time: **10** Minutes

Cook Time: **10** Minutes

Total Time: **20** Minutes

INGREDIENTS

- **3 ears corn**
- **1 tablespoon lemon zest**
- **1 tablespoon lemon juice**
- **½ cup butter**
- **1 tablespoon honey**
- **¼ tsp salt**
- **½ tsp pepper**
- **1 cup quinoa**
- **3 scallions**

DIRECTIONS

1. **In a pot place the corn and fill the pan with water, bring to boil and cover for 5-6 minutes**
2. **Remove from pot and let it cool**
3. **In a bowl mix the rest of the ingredients for dressing: lemon juice, melted butter, lemon zest, honey, pepper**

4. Cook the quinoa in a pot, add scallions in a bowl with the dressing and toss well

5. Season with salt and serve

Serves: **4**
Prep Time: **10**   Minutes

Cook Time: **10**   Minutes

Total Time: **20**   Minutes

INGREDIENTS

- **2 tablespoons chia**
- **¾ cup rolled oats**
- **1 cup vanilla cashewmilk**
- **½ cup fresh blueberries**
- **2 strawberries**
- **½ raspberries**
- **sprinkle of granola**

DIRECTIONS

1. **In a bowl mix cashewmilk, oats, chia and divide into 2 servings**
2. **Refrigerate overnight, remove top with berries and serve**

OVERNIGHT OATS

Serves: 2

Prep Time: 5   Minutes

Cook Time: 5   Minutes

Total Time: 10   Minutes

INGREDIENTS

- 2 tablespoons chia
- ¾ cup rolled oats
- 1 cup vanilla cashewmilk
- ¼ cup peach
- ¼ plum
- 3 basil leaves
- 1 tsp pumpkin seeds
- 1 tsp hemp seeds

DIRECTIONS

1. In a bowl mix cashewmilk, oats, chia and oats, divide into 2-3 servings
2. Refrigerate overnight
3. Remove and serve

AVOCADO BROWNIE

Serves: **4**

Prep Time: **10**   Minutes

Cook Time: **30**   Minutes

Total Time: **40**   Minutes

INGREDIENTS

- **1 ripe avocado**
- **3 tablespoons melted butter**
- **1 egg**
- **¼ cup brown sugar**
- **¼ maple syrup**
- **1 tablespoon vanilla extract**
- **¾ cup cocoa powder**
- **½ tsp salt**
- **½ cup gluten-free flour**
- **¼ cup dark chocolate chips**

DIRECTIONS

1. **Preheat the oven to 325 F**
2. **In a bowl mash the avocado, brown sugar, maple syrup, vanilla, sugar, water, butter, add cocoa powder**
3. **In a bowl mix salt and flour and stir in avocado mixture, spread bake in the pan and bake for 35 minutes**

4. Remove and cool before serving

BREAKFAST MIX

Serves: **1**
Prep Time: **5**   Minutes

Cook Time: **5**   Minutes

Total Time: **10**   Minutes

INGREDIENTS

- 1 cup corn cereal
- 1 cup rice cereal
- ¼ cup cocoa cereal
- ¼ cup rice cakes

DIRECTIONS

1. In a bowl combine all ingredients together
2. Serve with milk

SAUSAGE BREAKFAST SANDWICH

Serves: 2

Prep Time: 5   Minutes

Cook Time: 15   Minutes

Total Time: 20   Minutes

INGREDIENTS

- ¼ cup egg substitute
- 1 muffin
- 1 turkey sausage patty
- 1 tablespoon cheddar cheese

DIRECTIONS

1. In a skillet pour egg and cook on low heat
2. Place turkey sausage patty in a pan and cook for 4-5 minutes per side
3. On a toasted muffin place the cooked egg, top with a sausage patty and cheddar cheese
4. Serve when ready

BREAKFAST GRANOLA

Serves: 2

Prep Time: 5   Minutes

Cook Time: **30**   Minutes

Total Time: **35**   Minutes

INGREDIENTS

- 1 tsp vanilla extract
- 1 tablespoon honey
- 1 lb. rolled oats
- 2 tablespoons sesame seeds
- ¼ lb. almonds
- ¼ lb. berries

DIRECTIONS

1. Preheat the oven to 325 F
2. Spread the granola onto a baking sheet
3. Bake for 12-15 minutes, remove and mix everything
4. Bake for another 12-15 minutes or until slightly brown
5. When ready remove from the oven and serve

RASPBERRY CRUMBLE

Serves: **4**

Prep Time: **10** Minutes

Cook Time: **50** Minutes

Total Time: **60** Minutes

INGREDIENTS

- 2 eggs
- 1 cup raspberries
- 1 cup apple juice
- 1 cup oats
- 1 tablespoon butter
- 1 tablespoon brown sugar
- 1 tablespoon cinnamon
- ¼ tsp cloves

DIRECTIONS

1. Preheat oven to 375 F
2. In a bowl combine raspberries, apple slices and apple juice
3. In another bowl combine sugar, spices, oats, butter and mix well
4. Cover apple slices with crumble topping
5. Bake for 45-50 minutes
6. When ready remove and serve

QUINOA CREPES WITH APPLESAUCE

Serves: **4**

Prep Time: **10** Minutes

Cook Time: **30** Minutes

Total Time: **40** Minutes

INGREDIENTS

- **1 cup quinoa flour**
- **½ cup tapioca flour**
- **1 tsp baking soda**
- **1 tsp cinnamon**
- **1 cup water**
- **2 tablespoons canola oil**
- **2 cups organic apple sauce**

DIRECTIONS

1. **In a bowl combine quinoa flour, baking soda, cinnamon, tapioca flour, water, oil and whisk well**
2. **Preheat a skillet over medium heat and pour ¼ cup batter into skillet**
3. **Cook each crepe on low heat for 1-2 minutes per side**
4. **When ready remove and serve with apple sauce**

CHEESE OMELETTE

Serves: *1*
Prep Time: 5   Minutes

Cook Time: *10*   Minutes

Total Time: *15*   Minutes

INGREDIENTS

- 2 eggs
- ¼ tsp salt
- ¼ tsp black pepper
- 1 tablespoon olive oil
- ¼ cup cheese
- ¼ tsp basil
- 1 cup low-fat cheese

DIRECTIONS

1. In a bowl combine all ingredients together and mix well
2. In a skillet heat olive oil and pour the egg mixture
3. Cook for 1-2 minutes per side
4. When ready remove omelette from the skillet and serve

CUCUMBER OMELETTE

Serves: **1**

Prep Time: **5** Minutes

Cook Time: **10** Minutes

Total Time: **15** Minutes

INGREDIENTS

- 2 eggs
- ¼ tsp salt
- ¼ tsp black pepper
- 1 tablespoon olive oil
- ¼ cup cheese
- ¼ tsp basil
- 1 cup cucumber

DIRECTIONS

1. In a bowl combine all ingredients together and mix well
2. In a skillet heat olive oil and pour the egg mixture
3. Cook for 1-2 minutes per side
4. When ready remove omelette from the skillet and serve

PANCAKES

BANANA PANCAKES

Serves: **4**

Prep Time: **10** Minutes

Cook Time: **20** Minutes

Total Time: **30** Minutes

INGREDIENTS

- 1 cup whole wheat flour
- ¼ tsp baking soda
- ¼ tsp baking powder
- 1 cup mashed banana
- 2 eggs
- 1 cup milk

DIRECTIONS

1. In a bowl combine all ingredients together and mix well
2. In a skillet heat olive oil
3. Pour ¼ of the batter and cook each pancake for 1-2 minutes per side
4. When ready remove from heat and serve

BUCKWHEAT PANCAKES

Serves: *6*
Prep Time: *5*   Minutes

Cook Time: *10*   Minutes

Total Time: *15*   Minutes

INGREDIENTS

- 1 cup buckwheat flour
- 1 tablespoon brown sugar
- ¼ tsp salt
- 1 tsp baking powder
- 1 cup almond milk
- 1 tablespoon canola oil
- 2 bananas

DIRECTIONS

1. In a bowl combine dry ingredients
2. Add wet ingredients and mix well
3. In a skillet pour ¼ cup batter and cook for 1-2 minutes per side
4. When ready remove and serve with syrup

COOKIES

MORNING COOKIES

Serves: **6**

Prep Time: **10** Minutes

Cook Time: **15** Minutes

Total Time: **25** Minutes

INGREDIENTS

- **3 bananas**
- **¼ cup peanut butter**
- **¼ cup cocoa powder**
- **handful of salt**

DIRECTIONS

1. **Preheat oven to 325 F**
2. **In a bowl mix all ingredients**
3. **Form small cookies and place them onto a greased cookie sheet**
4. **Sprinkle with salt and bake for 12-15 minutes**
5. **Remove and serve**

Serves: *8*
Prep Time: *5*   Minutes

Cook Time: *30*   Minutes

Total Time: *35*   Minutes

INGREDIENTS

- **2 cups oats**
- **½ tsp cinnamon**
- **1 cup blueberries**
- **½ cup honey**
- **½ cup almond butter**
- **1 tsp vanilla**

DIRECTIONS

1. **Mix all of the ingredients together, except for the blueberries.**
2. **Fold in the blueberries and refrigerate for 30 minutes.**
3. **Form balls from the mixture and serve.**

GINGER LEMONADE

Serves: *8*

Prep Time: *5*   Minutes

Cook Time: *10*   Minutes

Total Time: *15*   Minutes

INGREDIENTS

- 1/3 cup honey
- 4 lemons juice
- Ice
- 4 strips of lemon peel
- 2 tbs ginger root
- 2 sprigs rosemary

DIRECTIONS

1. Mix the honey, ginger, lemon peel and 2 sprigs rosemary in a pot with 2 cups water.
2. Bring to a boil, then simmer for 10 minutes.
3. Remove from heat and allow to cool for 15 minutes.
4. Strain into a pitcher.
5. Discard the ginger and rosemary.
6. Add 6 cups of cold water and lemon juice to the pitcher.
7. Stir to combine and serve with ice.

LIME GRILLED CORN

Serves: **4**

Prep Time: **5** Minutes

Cook Time: **15** Minutes

Total Time: **20** Minutes

INGREDIENTS

- **4 corns**
- **2 tbs mayonnaise**
- **Salt**
- **Pepper**
- **2 tbs lime juice**
- **¼ tsp chili powder**

DIRECTIONS

1. **Preheat the grill.**
2. **Cook the shucked corn onto the grill for 5 minutes.**
3. **Turn every few minutes until all sides are charred.**
4. **Mix the mayonnaise, chili powder, and lime juice in a bowl.**
5. **Season with salt and pepper and add lime juice and chili powder.**
6. **Serve coated with the mayonnaise mixture.**

APPLE CRUMBLE

Serves: **6**

Prep Time: **10**   Minutes

Cook Time: **30**   Minutes

Total Time: **40**   Minutes

INGREDIENTS

- 4 apples
- 2 tsp cinnamon
- 1 cup flour
- ½ cup walnuts
- 2 cups quinoa
- 1/3 cup ground almonds

DIRECTIONS

1. Preheat the oven to 350F.
2. Oil a baking dish.
3. Place the apples into prepared dishes.
4. Mix the remaining ingredients in a bowl.
5. Crumble over the apples.
6. Bake for 30 minutes.
7. Serve immediately.

Serves: *18*

Prep Time: *10*   Minutes

Cook Time: *10*   Minutes

Total Time: *20*   Minutes

INGREDIENTS

- 1 ¾ cups flour
- 1 ¾ ground ginger
- ¼ tsp ground cinnamon
- 1/8 tsp nutmeg
- 1/8 tsp cloves
- 1 ½ tsp cornstarch
- ¼ cup milk
- ¼ cup molasses
- 3 tbs Swerve
- ¼ tsp salt
- 2 tbs butter
- 1 egg white
- 2 ¼ tsp vanilla
- 2 tsp stevia
- 1 tsp baking powder

DIRECTIONS

1. Preheat the oven to 325F.
2. Mix the cornstarch, nutmeg, flour, cloves, ginger, cinnamon, baking powder, and salt in a bowl.
3. In another bowl, whisk the butter, egg, vanilla, and stevia.
4. Stir in the molasses and milk.
5. Incorporate the flour mixture.
6. Divide into 18 portions and roll into balls.
7. Roll in the Swerve until coated.
8. Place on a lined baking sheet.
9. Sprinkle with Swerve and bake for 10 minutes.
10. Allow to cool, then serve.

Serves: **16**

Prep Time: **10**   Minutes

Cook Time: **60**   Minutes

Total Time: **70**   Minutes

INGREDIENTS

- **4 cups rice cereal**
- **2 tbs dark chocolate**
- **2/3 cup honey**
- **½ cup peanut butter**
- **Salt**
- **1 tsp vanilla**

DIRECTIONS

1. **Combine all of the ingredients except for the dark chocolate in a bowl.**
2. **Spread the mixture on a lined baking pan.**
3. **Drizzle the melted chocolate on top.**
4. **Refrigerate for 1 hour.**
5. **Cut into bars and serve.**

BREAKFAST COOKIES

Serves: **8-12**

Prep Time: **5** Minutes

Cook Time: **15** Minutes

Total Time: **20** Minutes

INGREDIENTS

- 1 cup rolled oats
- ¼ cup applesauce
- ½ tsp vanilla extract
- 3 tablespoons chocolate chips
- 2 tablespoons dried fruits
- 1 tsp cinnamon

DIRECTIONS

1. Preheat the oven to 325 F
2. In a bowl combine all ingredients together and mix well
3. Scoop cookies using an ice cream scoop
4. Place cookies onto a prepared baking sheet
5. Place in the oven for 12-15 minutes or until the cookies are done
6. When ready remove from the oven and serve

TANGERINE SMOOTHIE

Serves: *1*
Prep Time: *5*   Minutes

Cook Time: *5*   Minutes

Total Time: *10*   Minutes

INGREDIENTS

- 2 tangerines
- 1 cup pineapple
- 1 banana
- 1 cup ice

DIRECTIONS

1. In a blender place all ingredients and blend until smooth
2. Pour smoothie in a glass and serve

MOCKTAIL

Serves: **1**

Prep Time: **10** Minutes

Cook Time: **0** Minutes

Total Time: **10** Minutes

INGREDIENTS

- Ice
- 6 ounces soda water
- 3 lime slices
- 11 mint leaves
- 1 tbs honey

DIRECTIONS

1. Add mint leaves and lime to a glass and muddle with a spoon.
2. Add honey, ice and soda.
3. Stir to combine.
4. Serve garnished with lime and mint.

PEANUT BUTTER SMOOTHIE

Serves: *1*

Prep Time: *5*   Minutes

Cook Time: *5*   Minutes

Total Time: *10*   Minutes

INGREDIENTS

- 1 cup strawberries
- 1 banana
- 2 tablespoons peanut butter

DIRECTIONS

1. In a blender place all ingredients and blend until smooth
2. Pour smoothie in a glass and serve

CARROT SMOOTHIE

Serves: *1*
Prep Time: 5   Minutes

Cook Time: 5   Minutes

Total Time: *10* Minutes

INGREDIENTS

- 1 carrot
- 1 mango
- 2 tablespoons coconut flakes

DIRECTIONS

1. **In a blender place all ingredients and blend until smooth**
2. **Pour smoothie in a glass and serve**

GINGER SMOOTHIE

Serves: *1*

Prep Time: *5*   Minutes

Cook Time: *5*   Minutes

Total Time: *10*   Minutes

INGREDIENTS

- 2 cups pineapple
- 2 tablespoons lime juice
- 1-pice ginger

DIRECTIONS

1. In a blender place all ingredients and blend until smooth
2. Pour smoothie in a glass and serve

KALE SMOOTHIE

Serves: *1*

Prep Time: 5   Minutes

Cook Time: 5   Minutes

Total Time: *10* Minutes

INGREDIENTS

- 1 cup kale
- 1 cup cherries
- 1 cup blueberries

DIRECTIONS

1. In a blender place all ingredients and blend until smooth
2. Pour smoothie in a glass and serve

MANGO SMOOTHIE

Serves: **1**

Prep Time: **5** Minutes

Cook Time: **5** Minutes

Total Time: **10** Minutes

INGREDIENTS

- 1 cup mango
- 1 cup cherries
- 1 cup Greek yogurt

DIRECTIONS

1. In a blender place all ingredients and blend until smooth
2. Pour smoothie in a glass and serve

MUFFINS

SIMPLE MUFFINS

Serves: **8-12**

Prep Time: **10**   Minutes

Cook Time: **20**   Minutes

Total Time: **30**   Minutes

INGREDIENTS

- 2 eggs
- 1 tablespoon olive oil
- 1 cup milk
- 2 cups whole wheat flour
- 1 tsp baking soda
- ¼ tsp baking soda
- 1 cup pumpkin puree
- 1 tsp cinnamon
- ¼ cup molasses

DIRECTIONS

1. In a bowl combine all wet ingredients
2. In another bowl combine all dry ingredients

3. Combine wet and dry ingredients together
4. Pour mixture into 8-12 prepared muffin cups, fill 2/3 of the cups
5. Bake for 18-20 minutes at 375 F
6. When ready remove from the oven and serve

CORNBREAD MUFFINS

Serves: **4**

Prep Time: **10** Minutes

Cook Time: **20** Minutes

Total Time: **30** Minutes

INGREDIENTS

- 1 cup whole-wheat flour
- 1 can of Whole Kernel Corn 15 oz.
- ½ cup milk
- 1 egg
- ½ cup butter
- 1 tablespoon honey
- 1 tablespoon baking powder
- 1 tsp salt

DIRECTIONS

1. Preheat oven to 375 F
2. Blend corn until smooth
3. In a bowl mix baking powder, salt and flour
4. In another bowl mix eggs, butter, corn, milk and honey
5. Pour over the flour mixture and mix well
6. Pour mixture into a cupcake pan and bake for 15-20 minutes

MORNING MUFFINS

Serves: *8-12*
Prep Time: *10*   Minutes

Cook Time: *25*   Minutes

Total Time: *35*   Minutes

INGREDIENTS

- 1 cup oats
- ¼ cup unsweetened applesauce
- 2 egg whites
- 1 cup oat milk
- 1 cup whole wheat flour
- ¼ cup brown sugar
- ¼ tsp baking soda
- ¼ tsp salt
- 1 tsp cinnamon
- ½ cup blueberries

DIRECTIONS

1. Preheat oven to 375 F
2. In a bowl combine all ingredients together and mix well
3. Fill 8-12 paper muffin cups with batter and fold in blueberries
4. Bake for 20-25 minutes, serve when ready

FIBER MUFFINS

Serves: **8-12**
Prep Time: **5**   Minutes

Cook Time: **15**   Minutes

Total Time: **20**   Minutes

INGREDIENTS

- 1 cup wheat bran
- 1cup nonfat milk
- ¼ cup unsweetened applesauce
- 1 egg
- ¼ cup brown sugar
- ¼ cup all-purpose flour
- ¼ cup whole wheat flour
- 1 tsp baking powder
- 1 tsp baking soda
- ¼ tsp salt
- 1 cup blueberries

DIRECTIONS

1. Preheat oven to 400 F
2. In a bowl combine wheat bran and milk and set aside
3. In another bowl combine egg, brown sugar, apple sauce and stir in bran mixture, mix well

4. In another bowl combine baking soda, baking powder, wheat flour, all-purpose flour and mix well

5. Stir flour mixture into bran and egg mixture and mix well

6. Fold in blueberries and fill muffin cups with batter

7. Bake for 12-15 minutes

8. When ready remove and serve

STRAWBERRY MUFFINS

Serves:	**8-12**
Prep Time:	**10** Minutes
Cook Time:	**20** Minutes
Total Time:	**30** Minutes

INGREDIENTS

- 2 eggs
- 1 tablespoon olive oil
- 1 cup milk
- 2 cups whole wheat flour
- 1 tsp baking soda
- ¼ tsp baking soda
- 1 tsp cinnamon
- 1 cup strawberries

DIRECTIONS

1. In a bowl combine all wet ingredients
2. In another bowl combine all dry ingredients
3. Combine wet and dry ingredients together
4. Fold in strawberries and mix well
5. Pour mixture into 8-12 prepared muffin cups, fill 2/3 of the cups
6. Bake for 18-20 minutes at 375 F, remove when ready

CHOCOLATE MUFFINS

Serves: *8-12*

Prep Time: *10*   Minutes

Cook Time: *20*   Minutes

Total Time: *30*   Minutes

INGREDIENTS

- 2 eggs
- 1 tablespoon olive oil
- 1 cup milk
- 2 cups whole wheat flour
- 1 tsp baking soda
- ¼ tsp baking soda
- 1 tsp cinnamon
- 1 cup chocolate chips

DIRECTIONS

1. In a bowl combine all wet ingredients
2. In another bowl combine all dry ingredients
3. Combine wet and dry ingredients together
4. Fold in chocolate chips and mix well
5. Pour mixture into 8-12 prepared muffin cups, fill 2/3 of the cups
6. Bake for 18-20 minutes at 375 F, remove when ready

SIMPLE MUFFINS

Serves: **8-12**
Prep Time: **10**   Minutes

Cook Time: **20**   Minutes

Total Time: **30**   Minutes

INGREDIENTS

- 2 eggs
- 1 tablespoon olive oil
- 1 cup milk
- 2 cups whole wheat flour
- 1 tsp baking soda
- ¼ tsp baking soda
- 1 tsp cinnamon

DIRECTIONS

1. In a bowl combine all wet ingredients
2. In another bowl combine all dry ingredients
3. Combine wet and dry ingredients together
4. Pour mixture into 8-12 prepared muffin cups, fill 2/3 of the cups
5. Bake for 18-20 minutes at 375 F
6. When ready remove from the oven and serve

THIRD COOKBOOK

PUMPKIN CUPCAKES

Serves: **4**

Prep Time: **10**   Minutes

Cook Time: **30**   Minutes

Total Time: **40**   Minutes

INGREDIENTS

- 1 cup pumpkin puree
- 1 tsp cinnamon
- ½ tsp mixed spice
- 1 tsp ginger
- ¼ lb. butter
- 1 cups brown sugar
- 2 eggs
- 2 cups flour
- 3 tsp baking powder

DIRECTIONS

1. Boil the pumpkin and then puree in a food processor
2. Cream butter and sugar, add the eggs and beat well, stir in pureed pumpkin and dry ingredients
3. Combine all ingredients and spoon mixture into a muffin tin

4. Bake at 300 F for 20 minutes, remove and serve

BUCKWHEAT PANCAKES

Serves: **2**

Prep Time: **10**   Minutes

Cook Time: **10**   Minutes

Total Time: **20**   Minutes

INGREDIENTS

- 1 cup buckwheat mix
- 1 egg
- 1 cup milk
- 1 tablespoon butter

DIRECTIONS

1. In a bow mix all ingredients, add olive oil and pour batter
2. Cook for 1-2 minutes per side
3. Remove and serve

CARROT CAKE

Serves: **4**

Prep Time: **10** Minutes

Cook Time: **40** Minutes

Total Time: **50** Minutes

INGREDIENTS

- 1 cup whole meal self raising flour
- 1 cup brown sugar
- 1 cup self raising flour
- 1 tsp salt
- 1 tsp cinnamon
- 1 tsp ginger
- 1 cup olive oil
- 2 cups carrots
- 3 eggs
- ½ tsp allspice

DIRECTIONS

1. Preheat oven to 275 F and place all ingredients in a bowl except eggs
2. In another bowl mix eggs and add to the mixture
3. Pour into cake in
4. For carrot cake pour batter into cupcake molds

5. Bake for 40 minutes
6. Remove and serve

RUSSIAN FUDGE

Serves: **2**

Prep Time: **10**   Minutes

Cook Time: **30**   Minutes

Total Time: **40**   Minutes

INGREDIENTS

- ½ butter
- 1 can condensed milk
- ¾ cup milk
- 2 tablespoons golden syrup
- 3 cups sugar
- 1 tablespoon vanilla essence

DIRECTIONS

1. In a pot place all the ingredients except vanilla essence and bring to boil
2. Boil for 15-20 minutes and in another bowl drop some fudge mixture
3. Add vanilla essence and beat with a mixer for 5-6 minutes
4. Pour into greased tin and place in fridge
5. Cut into pieces and serve

Serves: **2**

Prep Time: **10** Minutes

Cook Time: **20** Minutes

Total Time: **30** Minutes

INGREDIENTS

- 1-inch ginger
- 4 tablespoons brown sugar
- 1 tsp citric acid
- 1 L soda water
- fresh mint

DIRECTIONS

1. Grate ginger and mix with the rest of ingredients and let them sit for 10-12 minutes
2. Serve when ready

CINNAMON SCONES

Serves: **4**

Prep Time: **10**   Minutes

Cook Time: **30**   Minutes

Total Time: **40**   Minutes

INGREDIENTS

- 2 cups self raising flour
- 2 tablespoons butter
- 2/3 cups milk

FILLING

- 1/3 cup butter
- ¾ cup brown sugar
- 1 tsp cinnamon

DIRECTIONS

1. Preheat oven to 350 F
2. In a blender add butter, flour and blend until smooth
3. Add milk and blend or another 1-2 minutes
4. Remove mixture onto floured surface
5. In the blender put all ingredients for the filling and blend until smooth
6. Spread the filling into the dough

Serves: **4**

Prep Time: **10**   Minutes

Cook Time: **30**   Minutes

Total Time: **40**   Minutes

INGREDIENTS

- 1 leek
- 1 clove garlic
- sat
- citric acid
- 1 tsp turmeric
- 1 tsp cumin
- 1 tsp coriander powder
- ½ cup roasted sunflower seeds
- 1 tablespoon rice flour
- 1 tsp arrowroot
- 1 cup broccoli
- 2 tablespoons butter
- 1 cup milk
- macaroni pasta

DIRECTIONS

1. Cook pasta, add leek and sauté with butter, citric acid and pepper
2. Add butter, cumin, coriander powder, turmeric, sunflower seeds
3. Add arrowroot and rice flour and cook for 2-3 minutes
4. Add broccoli, pasta and stir
5. Cook for 20 minutes at 350 F, remove and serve

SPRING ROLLS

Serves: *4*

Prep Time: *10*   Minutes

Cook Time: *20*   Minutes

Total Time: *30*   Minutes

INGREDIENTS

- rice noodles
- onion
- cucumber
- carrot
- Coriander
- zucchini
- carrot
- Thai mint
- Chives
- Roasted sunflower seeds
- ginger
- rice paper
- tofu

DIRECTIONS

1. **In a bowl place the noodles and boil, cover with a lid**

2. When they are cool set aside, soak a couple of rice papers in warm water and place the rice paper on a towel

3. Place the noodles and the rest of rest of ingredients on a rice paper and fold

4. Serve when ready

Serves: **4**

Prep Time: **10** Minutes

Cook Time: **30** Minutes

Total Time: **40** Minutes

INGREDIENTS

- ¼ lb. butter
- ½ cup sugar
- 1 cup plain flour
- ½ whole meal flour
- 1 tsp baking powder
- 1 tsp ginger

DIRECTIONS

1. In a food processor add butter and soon and blend until smooth
2. Add the rest of ingredients and blend
3. Remove from blender and bake for 20 minutes at 350 F
4. Cut into cookie shape and serve

Serves: **2**

Prep Time: **10** Minutes

Cook Time: **10** Minutes

Total Time: **20** Minutes

INGREDIENTS

- 1 cup corn flour
- 1 egg
- 1 cup milk
- 1 tablespoon butter
- 2 tablespoons honey
- ½ cup rice flour
- 1 tsp baking powder
- ½ tsp salt

DIRECTIONS

1. Let sit for 8-10 minutes
2. Place in the waffle iron and cook
3. Remove and serve

CHEESE CAKE

Serves: **4**

Prep Time: **10** Minutes

Cook Time: **30** Minutes

Total Time: **40** Minutes

INGREDIENTS

- ½ lb. gingernut biscuits
- ½ lb. blueberries
- 1 tsp vanilla extract
- 1 tsp acid
- ¼ lb. butter
- ¼ lb. caster sugar
- 2 tablespoons arrowroot
- ¼ lb. full-fat Philadelphia
- 2 eggs

DIRECTIONS

1. Preheat oven to 350 F
2. In a bowl mix butter and biscuits and press into the base of the tin
3. Bake for 10-12 minutes
4. In a saucepan cook blueberry with sugar and milk for 10-12 minutes

5. Take off heat add citric acid and vanilla
6. Bake for 40 minutes remove and let it chill

BASIC WAFFLES

Serves: **2**

Prep Time: **10**   Minutes

Cook Time: **10**   Minutes

Total Time: **20**   Minutes

INGREDIENTS

- 2 eggs
- 1 tablespoon sugar
- 1 tablespoon baking powder
- 1 cup flour
- 1/8 cup milk
- ½ tsp vanilla essence

DIRECTIONS

1. **In a food processor add all the ingredients and blend until smooth**
2. **Heat the waffle iron pour in the batter**
3. **Cook until golden**
4. **Serve with maple syrup**

Serves: **4**

Prep Time: **10** Minutes

Cook Time: **20** Minutes

Total Time: **30** Minutes

INGREDIENTS

- 1 tablespoon olive oil
- 4 tablespoons popcorn kernels

CARAMEL SAUCE

- 1 tablespoon butter
- 1 tablespoon brown sugar
- 1 tablespoon golden syrup

DIRECTIONS

1. In a saucepan pour olive oil and popcorn kernels over medium heat and cover
2. Shake the saucepan to distribute evenly
3. In another saucepan melt the caramel sauce ingredients
4. Remove from heat and pour over your popcorn

Serves: **4**

Prep Time: **10** Minutes

Cook Time: **10** Minutes

Total Time: **20** Minutes

INGREDIENTS

- ½ tsp salt
- 1 cup plain flour
- 1 tsp olive oil
- 1 onion
- ½ cup hot water
- 1 tablespoon cold water

DIRECTIONS

1. In a bowl mix all ingredients
2. Pour mixture into a pan and cook for 1-2 minutes per side
3. Remove and serve

TOASTED MUESLI

Serves: **4**

Prep Time: **10**   Minutes

Cook Time: **60**   Minutes

Total Time: **70**   Minutes

INGREDIENTS

- 2 cups oats
- 1 cup oat mix
- ½ cup sunflower seeds
- ½ cup sunflower oil

DIRECTIONS

1. In a bowl mix all ingredients
2. Bake for 60 minutes at 275 F
3. Garnish with blueberries and serve

GINGERBREAD BISCUITS

Serves: **4**

Prep Time: **10** Minutes

Cook Time: **30** Minutes

Total Time: **40** Minutes

INGREDIENTS

- 2 oz. butter
- 1 cup self raising flour
- ½ tsp salt
- 3 tablespoons ginger
- ½ cup milk
- 1 egg beaten
- 1 tablespoon vanilla extract
- ½ cup golden syrup
- ½ cup maple syrup
- ½ cup honey

DIRECTIONS

1. Preheat oven to 300 F
2. In a pan melt honey, butter, syrup and set aside
3. White syrup mixture is cooling, grate the ginger and add to the syrup mixture
4. Add flour, salt, milk, egg and vanilla extract

117

5. Form small cookies and bake for 15-18 minutes at 300 F

6. Remove and serve

Serves: **4**

Prep Time: **10**   Minutes

Cook Time: **10**   Minutes

Total Time: **20**   Minutes

INGREDIENTS

- 2 cups hemp milk
- 2 packets stevia
- ½ tsp cinnamon
- ½ cup chia seeds
- 1 tablespoon vanilla extract

DIRECTIONS

1. In a bowl whisk all ingredients together
2. Let it chill overnight and serve

APPLE PANCAKES

Serves: **4**

Prep Time: **10**   Minutes

Cook Time: **20**   Minutes

Total Time: **30**   Minutes

INGREDIENTS

- 1 cup whole wheat flour
- ¼ tsp baking soda
- ¼ tsp baking powder
- 1 cup apples
- 2 eggs
- 1 cup milk

DIRECTIONS

1. In a bowl combine all ingredients together and mix well
2. In a skillet heat olive oil
3. Pour ¼ of the batter and cook each pancake for 1-2 minutes per side
4. When ready remove from heat and serve

Serves: **4**

Prep Time: **10**   Minutes

Cook Time: **30**   Minutes

Total Time: **40**   Minutes

INGREDIENTS

- 1 cup whole wheat flour
- ¼ tsp baking soda
- ¼ tsp baking powder
- 1 cup apricots
- 2 eggs
- 1 cup milk

DIRECTIONS

1. In a bowl combine all ingredients together and mix well
2. In a skillet heat olive oil
3. Pour ¼ of the batter and cook each pancake for 1-2 minutes per side
4. When ready remove from heat and serve

ACEROLA PANCAKES

Serves: *4*

Prep Time: *10*   Minutes

Cook Time: *20*   Minutes

Total Time: *30*   Minutes

INGREDIENTS

- 1 cup whole wheat flour
- ¼ tsp baking soda
- ¼ tsp baking powder
- 1 cup acerola
- 2 eggs
- 1 cup milk

DIRECTIONS

1. In a bowl combine all ingredients together and mix well
2. In a skillet heat olive oil
3. Pour ¼ of the batter and cook each pancake for 1-2 minutes per side
4. When ready remove from heat and serve

JAVA-PLUM MUFFINS

Serves: *8-12*

Prep Time: *10*   Minutes

Cook Time: *20*   Minutes

Total Time: *30*   Minutes

INGREDIENTS

- 2 eggs
- 1 tablespoon olive oil
- 1 cup milk
- 2 cups whole wheat flour
- 1 tsp baking soda
- ¼ tsp baking soda
- 1 tsp cinnamon
- 1 cup java-plum

DIRECTIONS

1. In a bowl combine all wet ingredients
2. In another bowl combine all dry ingredients
3. Combine wet and dry ingredients together
4. Pour mixture into 8-12 prepared muffin cups, fill 2/3 of the cups
5. Bake for 18-20 minutes at 375 F
6. When ready remove from the oven and serve

Serves: **8-12**

Prep Time: **10** Minutes

Cook Time: **20** Minutes

Total Time: **30** Minutes

INGREDIENTS

- 2 eggs
- 1 tablespoon olive oil
- 1 cup milk
- 2 cups whole wheat flour
- 1 tsp baking soda
- ¼ tsp baking soda
- 1 tsp cinnamon
- 1 cup kiwi

DIRECTIONS

1. In a bowl combine all wet ingredients
2. In another bowl combine all dry ingredients
3. Combine wet and dry ingredients together
4. Pour mixture into 8-12 prepared muffin cups, fill 2/3 of the cups
5. Bake for 18-20 minutes at 375 F
6. When ready remove from the oven and serve

CHOCOLATE MUFFINS

Serves: **8-12**

Prep Time: **10**   Minutes

Cook Time: **20**   Minutes

Total Time: **30**   Minutes

INGREDIENTS

- 2 eggs
- 1 tablespoon olive oil
- 1 cup milk
- 2 cups whole wheat flour
- 1 tsp baking soda
- ¼ tsp baking soda
- 1 tsp cinnamon
- 1 cup chocolate chips

DIRECTIONS

1. In a bowl combine all wet ingredients
2. In another bowl combine all dry ingredients
3. Combine wet and dry ingredients together
4. Pour mixture into 8-12 prepared muffin cups, fill 2/3 of the cups
5. Bake for 18-20 minutes at 375 F
6. When ready remove from the oven and serve

MANGO MUFFINS

Serves:	**8-12**
Prep Time:	**10** Minutes
Cook Time:	**20** Minutes
Total Time:	**30** Minutes

INGREDIENTS

- 2 eggs
- 1 tablespoon olive oil
- 1 cup milk
- 2 cups whole wheat flour
- 1 tsp baking soda
- ¼ tsp baking soda
- 1 tsp cinnamon
- 1 cup mango

DIRECTIONS

1. In a bowl combine all wet ingredients
2. In another bowl combine all dry ingredients
3. Combine wet and dry ingredients together
4. Pour mixture into 8-12 prepared muffin cups, fill 2/3 of the cups
5. Bake for 18-20 minutes at 375 F
6. When ready remove from the oven and serve

Serves: **1**

Prep Time: **5** Minutes

Cook Time: **10** Minutes

Total Time: **15** Minutes

INGREDIENTS

- 2 eggs
- ¼ tsp salt
- ¼ tsp black pepper
- 1 tablespoon olive oil
- ¼ cup cheese
- ¼ tsp basil
- 1 cup bok choy

DIRECTIONS

1. In a bowl combine all ingredients together and mix well
2. In a skillet heat olive oil and pour the egg mixture
3. Cook for 1-2 minutes per side
4. When ready remove omelette from the skillet and serve

BRUSSEL SPROUTS OMELETTE

Serves: **1**

Prep Time: **5**   Minutes

Cook Time: **10**   Minutes

Total Time: **15**   Minutes

INGREDIENTS

- 2 eggs
- ¼ tsp salt
- ¼ tsp black pepper
- 1 tablespoon olive oil
- ¼ cup cheese
- ¼ tsp basil
- 1 cup Brussel sprouts

DIRECTIONS

1. In a bowl combine all ingredients together and mix well
2. In a skillet heat olive oil and pour the egg mixture
3. Cook for 1-2 minutes per side
4. When ready remove omelette from the skillet and serve

CARROT OMELETTE

Serves: **1**

Prep Time: **5** Minutes

Cook Time: **10** Minutes

Total Time: **15** Minutes

INGREDIENTS

- 2 eggs
- ¼ tsp salt
- ¼ tsp black pepper
- 1 tablespoon olive oil
- ¼ cup cheese
- ¼ tsp basil
- 1 cup carrot

DIRECTIONS

1. In a bowl combine all ingredients together and mix well
2. In a skillet heat olive oil and pour the egg mixture
3. Cook for 1-2 minutes per side
4. When ready remove omelette from the skillet and serve

CORN OMELETTE

Serves: *1*
Prep Time: *5*   Minutes

Cook Time: *10*   Minutes

Total Time: *15*   Minutes

INGREDIENTS

- 2 eggs
- ¼ tsp salt
- ¼ tsp black pepper
- 1 tablespoon olive oil
- ¼ cup cheese
- ¼ tsp basil
- 1 cup corn

DIRECTIONS

1. In a bowl combine all ingredients together and mix well
2. In a skillet heat olive oil and pour the egg mixture
3. Cook for 1-2 minutes per side
4. When ready remove omelette from the skillet and serve

EGGPLANT OMELETTE

Serves: **1**

Prep Time: **5** Minutes

Cook Time: **10** Minutes

Total Time: **15** Minutes

INGREDIENTS

- 2 eggs
- ¼ tsp salt
- ¼ tsp black pepper
- 1 tablespoon olive oil
- ¼ cup cheese
- ¼ tsp basil
- 1 cup eggplant

DIRECTIONS

1. In a bowl combine all ingredients together and mix well
2. In a skillet heat olive oil and pour the egg mixture
3. Cook for 1-2 minutes per side
4. When ready remove omelette from the skillet and serve

TART RECIPES

APPLE TART

Serves: **6-8**

Prep Time: **25**   Minutes

Cook Time: **25**   Minutes

Total Time: **50**   Minutes

INGREDIENTS

- pastry sheets

FILLING

- 1 tsp lemon juice
- 3 oz. brown sugar
- 1 lb. apples
- 150 ml double cream
- 2 eggs

DIRECTIONS

1. Preheat oven to 400 F, unfold pastry sheets and place them on a baking sheet
2. Toss together all ingredients together and mix well
3. Spread mixture in a single layer on the pastry sheets
4. Before baking decorate with your desired fruits
5. Bake at 400 F for 22-25 minutes or until golden brown

6. When ready remove from the oven and serve

Serves:	**6-8**
Prep Time:	**25** Minutes
Cook Time:	**25** Minutes
Total Time:	**50** Minutes

INGREDIENTS

- pastry sheets
- 1 tsp vanilla extract
- ½ lb. caramel
- ½ lb. black chocolate
- 4-5 tablespoons butter
- 3 eggs
- ¼ lb. brown sugar

DIRECTIONS

1. Preheat oven to 400 F, unfold pastry sheets and place them on a baking sheet
2. Toss together all ingredients together and mix well
3. Spread mixture in a single layer on the pastry sheets
4. Before baking decorate with your desired fruits
5. Bake at 400 F for 22-25 minutes or until golden brown
6. When ready remove from the oven and serve

PIE RECIPES

PEACH PECAN PIE

Serves: **8-12**

Prep Time: **15**   Minutes

Cook Time: **35**   Minutes

Total Time: **50**   Minutes

INGREDIENTS

- 4-5 cups peaches
- 1 tablespoon preserves
- 1 cup sugar
- 4 small egg yolks
- ¼ cup flour
- 1 tsp vanilla extract

DIRECTIONS

1. Line a pie plate or pie form with pastry and cover the edges of the plate depending on your preference
2. In a bowl combine all pie ingredients together and mix well
3. Pour the mixture over the pastry
4. Bake at 400-425 F for 25-30 minutes or until golden brown
5. When ready remove from the oven and let it rest for 15 minutes

Serves: **8-12**

Prep Time: **15** Minutes

Cook Time: **35** Minutes

Total Time: **50** Minutes

INGREDIENTS

- pastry sheets
- 6-8 oz. chocolate crumb piecrust
- 1 cup half-and-half
- 1 package instant pudding mix
- 10-12 Oreo cookies
- 10 oz. whipped topping

DIRECTIONS

1. Line a pie plate or pie form with pastry and cover the edges of the plate depending on your preference
2. In a bowl combine all pie ingredients together and mix well
3. Pour the mixture over the pastry
4. Bake at 400-425 F for 25-30 minutes or until golden brown
5. When ready remove from the oven and let it rest for 15 minutes

GRAPEFRUIT PIE

Serves: **8-12**

Prep Time: **15**   Minutes

Cook Time: **35**   Minutes

Total Time: **50**   Minutes

INGREDIENTS

- pastry sheets
- 2 cups grapefruit
- 1 cup brown sugar
- ¼ cup flour
- 5-6 egg yolks
- 5 oz. butter

DIRECTIONS

1. Line a pie plate or pie form with pastry and cover the edges of the plate depending on your preference
2. In a bowl combine all pie ingredients together and mix well
3. Pour the mixture over the pastry
4. Bake at 400-425 F for 25-30 minutes or until golden brown
5. When ready remove from the oven and let it rest for 15 minutes

BUTTERFINGER PIE

Serves: **8-12**

Prep Time: **15** Minutes

Cook Time: **35** Minutes

Total Time: **50** Minutes

INGREDIENTS

- pastry sheets
- 1 package cream cheese
- 1 tsp vanilla extract
- ¼ cup peanut butter
- 1 cup powdered sugar (to decorate)
- 2 cups Butterfinger candy bars
- 8 oz whipped topping

DIRECTIONS

1. Line a pie plate or pie form with pastry and cover the edges of the plate depending on your preference
2. In a bowl combine all pie ingredients together and mix well
3. Pour the mixture over the pastry
4. Bake at 400-425 F for 25-30 minutes or until golden brown
5. When ready remove from the oven and let it rest for 15 minutes

CREAMSICLE SMOOTHIE

Serves: *1*
Prep Time: 5   Minutes

Cook Time: 5   Minutes

Total Time: *10*   Minutes

INGREDIENTS

- 2 cups mango
- 1 carrot
- 1 tablespoon apple cider vinegar
- 1 tsp lemon juice
- 1 cup coconut milk
- 1 tsp honey

DIRECTIONS

1. In a blender place all ingredients and blend until smooth
2. Pour smoothie in a glass and serve

BUTTERMILK SMOOTHIE

Serves: *1*
Prep Time: 5   Minutes

Cook Time: 5   Minutes

Total Time: *10*   Minutes

INGREDIENTS

- 1 cup strawberries
- 1 cup buttermilk
- 1 cup ice
- 1 tsp honey
- 1 tsp agave syrup

DIRECTIONS

1. In a blender place all ingredients and blend until smooth
2. Pour smoothie in a glass and serve

PARSLEY & PINEAPPLE SMOOTHIE

Serves: *1*
Prep Time: *5*   Minutes

Cook Time: *5*   Minutes

Total Time: *10* Minutes

INGREDIENTS

- 1 banana
- 1 cup pineapple
- ¼ cup parsley
- 1 tsp chia seeds
- 1 cup ice

DIRECTIONS

1. In a blender place all ingredients and blend until smooth
2. Pour smoothie in a glass and serve

POMEGRANATE SMOOTHIE

Serves: **1**

Prep Time: **5** Minutes

Cook Time: **5** Minutes

Total Time: **10** Minutes

INGREDIENTS

- 1 cup pomegranate juice
- ¼ cup vanilla yogurt
- 3 cooked beets
- ¼ cup grapefruit juice
- 1 tablespoon honey
- 1 cup ice

DIRECTIONS

1. In a blender place all ingredients and blend until smooth
2. Pour smoothie in a glass and serve

CASHEW SMOOTHIE

Serves: *1*

Prep Time: 5   Minutes

Cook Time: 5   Minutes

Total Time: *10*   Minutes

INGREDIENTS

- 1 cup cashew milk
- 1 cup vanilla yogurt
- 1 banana
- 1 cup pumpkin puree
- 1 cup ice

DIRECTIONS

1. In a blender place all ingredients and blend until smooth
2. Pour smoothie in a glass and serve

ICE-CREAM RECIPES

PISTACHIOS ICE-CREAM

Serves: **6-8**

Prep Time: **15**   Minutes

Cook Time: **15**   Minutes

Total Time: **30**   Minutes

INGREDIENTS

- 4 egg yolks
- 1 cup heavy cream
- 1 cup milk
- 1 cup sugar
- 1 vanilla bean
- 1 tsp almond extract
- 1 cup cherries
- ½ cup pistachios

DIRECTIONS

1. In a saucepan whisk together all ingredients
2. Mix until bubbly
3. Strain into a bowl and cool
4. Whisk in favorite fruits and mix well
5. Cover and refrigerate for 2-3 hours

6. Pour mixture in the ice-cream maker and follow manufacturer instructions
7. Serve when ready

VANILLA ICE-CREAM

Serves: **6-8**

Prep Time: **15**   Minutes

Cook Time: **15**   Minutes

Total Time: **30**   Minutes

INGREDIENTS

- 1 cup milk
- 1 tablespoon cornstarch
- 1 oz. cream cheese
- 1 cup heavy cream
- 1 cup brown sugar
- 1 tablespoon corn syrup
- 1 vanilla bean

DIRECTIONS

1. In a saucepan whisk together all ingredients
2. Mix until bubbly
3. Strain into a bowl and cool
4. Whisk in favorite fruits and mix well
5. Cover and refrigerate for 2-3 hours
6. Pour mixture in the ice-cream maker and follow manufacturer instructions
7. Serve when ready

THANK YOU FOR READING THIS BOOK!